UNDERSTANDING THE LIMITS OF ARTIFICIAL INTELLIGENCE FOR WARFIGHTERS

VOLUME 3_ PREDICTIVE MAINTENANCE

LI ANG ZHANG

YUSUF ASHPARI

ANTHONY JACQUES

PREPARED FOR THE DEPARTMENT OF THE AIR FORCE
APPROVED FOR PUBLIC RELEASE; DISTRIBUTION IS UNLIMITED.

 PROJECT AIR FORCE

03

For more information on this publication, visit **www.rand.org/t/RRA1722-3**.

About RAND

RAND is a research organization that develops solutions to public policy challenges to help make communities throughout the world safer and more secure, healthier and more prosperous. RAND is nonprofit, nonpartisan, and committed to the public interest. To learn more about RAND, visit www.rand.org.

Research Integrity

Our mission to help improve policy and decisionmaking through research and analysis is enabled through our core values of quality and objectivity and our unwavering commitment to the highest level of integrity and ethical behavior. To help ensure our research and analysis are rigorous, objective, and nonpartisan, we subject our research publications to a robust and exacting quality-assurance process; avoid both the appearance and reality of financial and other conflicts of interest through staff training, project screening, and a policy of mandatory disclosure; and pursue transparency in our research engagements through our commitment to the open publication of our research findings and recommendations, disclosure of the source of funding of published research, and policies to ensure intellectual independence. For more information, visit www.rand.org/about/research-integrity.

RAND's publications do not necessarily reflect the opinions of its research clients and sponsors.

Published by the RAND Corporation, Santa Monica, Calif.
© 2024 RAND Corporation
RAND® is a registered trademark.

Library of Congress Cataloging-in-Publication Data is available for this publication.

ISBN: 978-1-9774-1280-5

Cover: SSgt William Hopper/U.S. Air National Guard and Siarhei/Adobe Stock.

About This Report

This is the third report in a five-volume series addressing how artificial intelligence (AI) could be employed to assist warfighters in four distinct areas: cybersecurity, predictive maintenance, wargames, and mission planning. These areas were chosen to reflect the wide variety of potential uses and to highlight different kinds of limits to AI application. Each use case is presented in a separate volume, as it will be of interest to a different community.

This third volume assesses the appropriateness of statistical distributions for predicting airplane part failure and evaluates how AI can be used to determine the content of readiness spares packages (RSPs). It is aimed at those with an interest in predictive maintenance, RSPs, and AI applications more generally. Volume 1 in the series provides a summary of the findings and recommendations from all use cases, and the other volumes provide detailed analysis of the individual use cases:

- Lance Menthe, Li Ang Zhang, Edward Geist, Joshua Steier, Aaron B. Frank, Eric Van Hegewald, Gary J. Briggs, Keller Scholl, Yusuf Ashpari, and Anthony Jacques, *Understanding the Limits of Artificial Intelligence for Warfighters:* Vol. 1, *Summary*, RR-A1722-1, 2024
- Joshua Steier, Erik Van Hegewald, Anthony Jacques, Gavin S. Hartnett, and Lance Menthe, *Understanding the Limits of Artificial Intelligence for Warfighters:* Vol. 2, *Distributional Shift in Cybersecurity Datasets*, RR-A1722-2, 2024
- Edward Geist, Aaron B. Frank, and Lance Menthe, *Understanding the Limits of Artificial Intelligence for Warfighters:* Vol. 4, *Wargames*, RR-A1722-4, 2024
- Keller Scholl, Gary J. Briggs, Li Ang Zhang, and John L. Salmon, *Understanding the Limits of Artificial Intelligence for Warfighters:* Vol. 5, *Mission Planning*, RR-A1722-5, 2024.

The research reported here was commissioned by Air Force Materiel Command, Strategic Plans, Programs, Requirements and Assessments (AFMC/A5/8/9) and conducted within the Force Modernization and Employment Program of RAND Project AIR FORCE as part of a fiscal year 2022 project, "Understanding the Bounds of Artificial Intelligence in Warfare Applications."

RAND Project AIR FORCE

RAND Project AIR FORCE (PAF), a division of the RAND Corporation, is the Department of the Air Force's (DAF's) federally funded research and development center for studies and analyses, supporting both the United States Air Force and the United States Space Force. PAF provides the DAF with independent analyses of policy alternatives affecting the development, employment, combat readiness, and support of current and future air, space, and cyber forces. Research is conducted in four programs: Strategy and Doctrine; Force Modernization and Employment; Resource Management; and Workforce, Development, and Health. The research reported here was prepared under contract FA7014-22-D0001.

Additional information about PAF is available on our website:
www.rand.org/paf/

This report documents work originally shared with the DAF on September 23, 2022. The draft report, dated September 2022, was reviewed by formal peer reviewers and DAF subject-matter experts.

Acknowledgments

We thank our sponsor contact, Kathryn Sowers, and our action officers, Julia Phillips and Gregory Cazzell, for their guidance in choosing the use cases, for their thoughtfulness in scoping the research questions, and for working diligently with us to obtain the data necessary to conduct the many machine-learning experiments described in this series of reports. Thanks as well to the following individuals: Jeremy Brogdon for his assistance in obtaining and understanding predictive maintenance issues, Richard Moore for sharing his immense expertise in these matters, and R. Scott Erwin and Jean-Charles Ledé for graciously connecting us with many AI development efforts across the Air Force Research Laboratory. We also thank Brent Maxwell and the people on his team for helping us with the data and Rob Kline for speaking to us at length about the prediction challenges for spare parts.

We are also grateful to many current and former RAND colleagues, including Caolionn O'Connell, Sherrill Lingel, Osonde Osoba, and Chris Pernin for helping us shape the research agenda. Thanks to John Salmon for sharing his insights and to John Drew and James Leftwich for offering their invaluable expertise on predictive maintenance issues. We also thank Jair Aguirre and Abdel-Moez E. Bayoumi for reviewing this report and providing helpful feedback concerning its methods, content, and readability. We could not have written these reports without their help; any errors that remain are ours alone.

Summary

Issue

The U.S. Air Force (USAF) deploys flying units with readiness spares packages (RSPs) to try to ensure that the units are stocked with enough parts to be self-sufficient for 30 days. Predicting which parts are likely to fail—and, therefore, which parts should be included in the RSPs—is important because overstocking can be expensive and understocking can threaten mission readiness. In this report, we consider whether and when artificial intelligence (AI) methods could be used to improve RSP failure analysis, which currently assumes a probability distribution.

Approach

To test how AI might apply, we developed several machine-learning models and tested them on historical data to compare their performance with the optimization and prediction software currently employed. Using A-10C aircraft data as a test case, we addressed the following research questions:

- How does the current RSP failure analysis approach perform in a retrospective analysis against historical data?
- How can AI help inform the failure analysis process, and what are its limitations?
- What other potential improvements can augment the existing approach?

Key Findings

- **AI can improve failure analysis for RSPs on a case-by-case basis.** The current probability-based prediction process is a poor predictor of the performance of many parts. AI not only made better predictions but also, as a result, was much more cost effective. Figure S.1 shows one example of the performance of an AI model versus the current process. Updating the current prediction process with data can achieve a performance level that is quite close to that of our AI model.
- **It is necessary to establish a complex and labor-intensive data operations pipeline to USAF maintenance databases before any large-scale AI implementation can occur.** Historical data are essential to train and test AI models, but pulling these data from the relevant systems is a complex, manual process that involves scripting, drop-down lists, and nested menus. Moreover, considerable data cleaning is also needed. Given this situation, leveraging AI is practical only as a proof-of-concept model.
- **AI cannot alleviate the scarcity of wartime data.** It is unclear whether RSPs developed using peacetime data will be adequate for wartime operations. Moreover, one of the main limitations

of AI for this application is its inability to estimate truly rare events, which might be more likely during wartime operations. As a result, different approaches to modeling AI could be required to deal with these changing circumstances. However, regular retraining and updating, which is possible with an AI model, can ensure the adaptability of these models during wartime.

Figure S.1. Comparison of Actual Part Failure Rates for the A-10C Aircraft from 2007–2022 with Predictions by a Current Method and an Artificial Intelligence Model

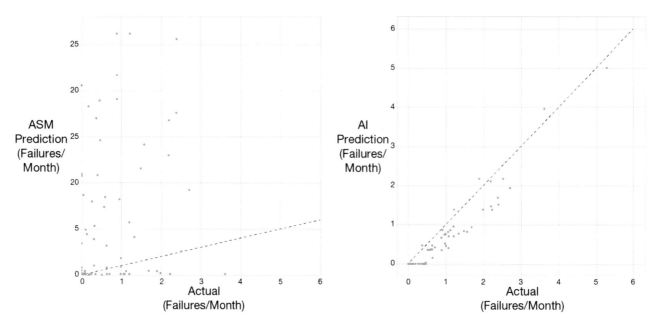

NOTE: ASM = Aircraft Sustainability Model. The dotted red line indicates parity in both subplots: If all predictions were accurate, they would all fall on the dotted red lines. The apparent slope of the dotted line is different because the scales of the two charts differ. The AI model (right) better aligns with actual failures per month but tends toward underpredictions. Given the rare nature of failures, high-accuracy predictions are not possible. The AI model predicts within ⊠2 of actual failures per month.

Recommendations for Air Force Materiel Command

- **Work with USAF Logistics (A4) to build a data operations pipeline to conduct retrospective analysis of aircraft maintenance and RSP efficiency.** Aircraft maintenance programs and databases function effectively for the purposes for which they were designed, but they were not designed for retrospective analysis or to train AI models. Automation of this data pipeline process could be necessary to make these data pulls before AI can be applied. Without these data, none of the following recommendations can be implemented.

- **Experiment with AI to improve failure analysis for RSPs.** Use the data pipeline to extend the proof-of-concept models to all aircraft. We noted subsets of aircraft parts where AI performs poorly. The analysis will likely have to be done on a part-by-part, platform-by-platform basis. Although it is difficult to determine whether AI (versus traditional methods) will perform better during war, AI does give logisticians another prediction tool.

- **Limit AI to failure analysis within the RSP process.** ASM software tackles the large and complex operations research problem of which parts to send from which depot to which base. Current AI capabilities are data hungry and are better suited to solving narrowly scoped problems.

Contents

About This Report...iii

Summary...v

Figures and Tables...ix

CHAPTER 1..1
Introduction...1
    Overview...1
    Readiness Spares Packages..1
    Approach...3
    Organization of This Report...3

CHAPTER 2..4
Aircraft Sustainability Model Failure Analysis Calculations...4
    Calculation of Readiness Spares Packages..4
    Assessment of Readiness Spares Package Modeling Assumptions...6
    Areas to Explore for Improvements by Artificial Intelligence...10

CHAPTER 3..11
Assessing the Potential for Artificial Intelligence..11
    Developing Performance Metrics..11
    Performance of Machine-Learning Algorithms...14
    Summary...18

CHAPTER 4..20
Challenges in Collecting and Preparing Maintenance Data for Artificial Intelligence........................20

CHAPTER 5..22
Summary of Findings and Recommendations..22
    Findings..22
    Recommendations for Air Force Materiel Command..23

APPENDIX A...24
In-Depth Methodology for Deriving Parts Failure Data from LIMS-EV and Other Supporting
    Information...24

APPENDIX B...31
Exploratory Analysis Using Days to Failure as a Predictor of Failure..31

Abbreviations...35
References...36

Figures and Tables

Figures

Figure S.1. Comparison of Actual Part Failure Rates for the A-10C Aircraft from 2007–2022 with Predictions by a Current Method and an Artificial Intelligence Model vi

Figure 1.1. The Nonconsumable Spares Process 2

Figure 2.1. How the Aircraft Sustainability Model Calculates Readiness Spares Package Composition............. 5

Figure 2.2. Comparison of Empirical Failure Rates to the Aircraft Sustainability Model Failure Rate Parameters 9

Figure 3.1. Updated Poisson Monthly Performance for the A-10C Readiness Spares Package Kit.................... 13

Figure 3.2. Artificial Intelligence Training and Testing Scheme 14

Figure 3.3. Neural Network Architectures Evaluated 15

Figure 3.4. Performance of a Linear Regression Model to Predict Failure Rates...................................... 16

Figure 3.5. Performance of a Regression Neural Network with Long Short-Term Memory to Predict Failure Rates 17

Figure 3.6. Performance of an Adjusted Regression Neural Network with Long Short-Term Memory to Predict Failure Rates 18

Figure 4.1. Deriving Empirical Part Failures from LIMS-EV Data 20

Figure B.1. Scatterplot of Predicted Days Versus True Days to Failure (All Data) 33

Tables

Table B.1. Boundary Comparison: Days to Failure 33

Table B.2. Boundary Comparison: Flying Hours to Failure... 34

Chapter 1

Introduction

Overview

The Department of the Air Force has become increasingly interested in the potential for artificial intelligence (AI) to revolutionize different aspects of warfighting. For this project, the U.S. Air Force (USAF) asked RAND Project AIR FORCE researchers to consider broadly what AI can and *cannot* do in order to understand the limits of AI for warfighting applications. To address this request, we investigated the applicability of AI to four specific warfighting applications: *cybersecurity*, *predictive maintenance*, *wargames*, and *mission planning*.

This report discusses the application of AI to predictive maintenance: how AI can augment failure analysis and its limitations.[1]

Readiness Spares Packages

The USAF provides flying units with spare parts to ensure that aircraft can remain mission-capable despite part failures. During a contingency or conflict, the USAF assumes that it will take 30 days for supply lines from the continental United States to be established. As a result, deployed units are provided with a spares kit, called a readiness spares package (RSP), to ensure that they are stocked with enough parts to be self-sufficient for 30 days. In general, parts are categorized as consumable or nonconsumable/repairable; RSPs are intended to supply units with repairable parts, which are usually rare (low inventory) and expensive items.

Filling RSPs involves predicting how many spares each unit will need to satisfy a given 30 days of sorties. Predictive maintenance plays a key role here: Predicting the right mix of spare parts to include in each RSP matters because overstocking can be expensive and understocking can threaten mission readiness. The USAF faces significant data challenges that hamper efforts to make predictions. There are significantly more peacetime flying hours in recent years than contingency flying hours, which could result in differing part failure rates. Furthermore, historical failures of such parts (either in peacetime or contingency) are usually rare. In this report, we use the RSP as a predictive maintenance case study to explore how well the current RSP process works and the potential for AI to improve it.

---

[1] In this report, we follow prior RAND Corporation researcher practice and consider AI to consist of six specific capabilities: (1) *computer vision*, the detection and classification of objects in visual media; (2) *natural language processing*, the recognition and translation of speech and text; planning, the use of models to find actions that lead to goals; (3) *prediction and classification*, the categorization of current and future data using prior data; generative learning, the synthesis of language, images, and other media; and (4) *expert systems*, rules-based models constructed to reflect expert knowledge and general heuristics (Stuart Russell and Peter Norvig, *Artificial Intelligence: A Modern Approach*, 3rd ed., Prentice Hall, 2010; Leila Wehbe and Aaditya Ramdas, "Introduction to Machine Learning," lecture notes, Carnegie Mellon University, Spring 2019).

The RSP process is complex because there are many depots and bases involved, each with its own inventory, supply, and demand for a vast number of spare parts across each aircraft series. A simplified view of this process is shown in Figure 1.1.

Figure 1.1. The Nonconsumable Spares Process

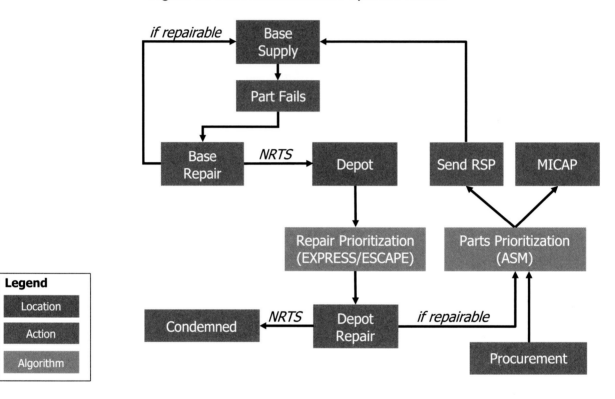

NOTE: ASM = Aircraft Sustainability Model; ESCAPE = Enterprise Supply Chain Analysis, Planning, and Execution; EXPRESS = Execution and Prioritization of Repair Support System; MICAP = mission impaired capability, awaiting parts; NRTS = not repairable this station.

Beginning at the top of Figure 1.1, if an aircraft part breaks, it generates a demand on the base's supply. If a spare is available, it will be installed on the plane. If not, the aircraft cannot fly and is considered "mission impaired capability, awaiting parts" (MICAP). Meanwhile, the broken part enters base repair, where it will be repaired or deemed "not repairable this station" (NRTS). NRTS parts are sent to the depot, where the Execution and Prioritization of Repair Support System (EXPRESS) prioritizes parts for induction and repair using the depot's manpower, resources, and open workbenches. If repair is possible, the part is added to the depot supply and awaits distribution to a base—otherwise, the part is condemned.[2]

ASM is the software that governs where parts in the depot supply are allocated. Generally, RSPs command a high priority of depot parts; typically, the parts are first used to fix MICAPs (i.e., filling

---

[2] At the time of this writing, EXPRESS was slated to be replaced by ESCAPE.

existing holes on the aircraft) and then allocated toward filling RSPs.[3] We will be looking specifically at how AI can (or cannot) improve the algorithms in Figure 1.1 (the blue boxes).

Approach

In the RSP process shown in Figure 1.1, repair prioritization and parts prioritization are two software-dependent processes that use optimization and prediction; these are the most straightforward applications for AI in this process. To test how AI might apply, we developed several machine-learning models and tested them on historical data to compare their performance with the optimization and prediction software currently employed for this purpose. As part of this process, we interviewed USAF and Air Force Sustainment Center (AFSC) subject-matter experts between September 2021 and May 2022 by phone and video call. The interviews were not for attribution, so no names are provided. Additional detail on the specific databases and machine-learning approaches that we used will be described later.

We encountered multiple challenges in acquiring data for this study. Once we obtained the data, time and resources constrained our analysis to the parts prioritization process governed by ASM. Using AI for other parts of the RSP process, such as assessing part reparability, performing part repair, and shipping or procuring parts, are also potentially valuable uses but were not considered in this study.[4] Using A-10C aircraft data as a test case, we addressed the following research questions:

- How does the current RSP failure analysis approach perform in a retrospective analysis against historical data?
- How can AI help inform the failure analysis process, and what are its limitations?
- What other potential improvements can augment the existing approach?

Organization of This Report

In Chapter 2, we assess the current process that ASM uses to calculate RSPs, understand its prediction capabilities, and evaluate the modeling assumptions involved. In Chapter 3, we use empirical part failure data to develop several neural networks, assess their performance, and identify their limitations. In Chapter 4, we document the challenges of collecting and processing USAF maintenance data for AI. In Chapter 5, we conclude with a summary of findings and recommendations.

---

[3] There are higher priority designations for spares, such as a Joint Chief of Staff project code, but they were not considered in this study.

[4] Autonomous vehicles or robotics could assist with the listed tasks, but assessments of those technologies have been left for separate studies. Assessing part reparability does not appear to exist yet as an AI capability, but current technology suggests its feasibility. For example, auto insurance companies are beginning to use AI to estimate car repair costs. See Aarian Marshall, "AI Comes to Car Repair, and Body Shop Owners Aren't Happy," *Wired*, April 13, 2021.

Chapter 2

Aircraft Sustainability Model Failure Analysis Calculations

In this chapter, we analyze how failure analysis is performed for RSPs, test the modeling assumptions involved, and establish a baseline performance for comparison with AI algorithms that we develop in Chapter 3. Given the myriad airframes that the USAF flies and the data processing challenges described in Chapter 4, we have limited our assessments to historical part failures on the A-10C.

Calculation of Readiness Spares Packages

The USAF currently uses ASM to calculate RSPs to maintain aircraft fleet availability and to manage maintenance budgets. ASM outputs a shopping list of parts for part managers to purchase for their RSPs. ASM was created by the Logistics Management Institute in the 1970s to calculate the composition of war reserve spares kits (WRSKs), the predecessor to RSPs.[5] ASM calculates the composition of RSPs to maximize aircraft availability across the fleet for a given budget. A summary of this process is shown in Figure 2.1.

---

[5] We learned during interviews that around the 1990s, the USAF changed the WRSK to the RSP in an enterprise-wide effort to remove wartime and peacetime earmarked limitations on spares. In the era of WRSKs, the USAF separately designated wartime spares from peacetime spares. Wartime spares were not allowed to be used to fill peacetime demand, barring colonel-level permission. The enterprise-level move toward RSPs consisted of a perspective change that a "spare is a spare," removing such designation distinctions and allowing RSPs to be used for peacetime demand. See also Douglas J. Blazer, "Updating Air Force War Planning for Spares Support," *Air Force Journal of Logistics*, Vol. 35, Nos. 3–4, Fall-Winter 2011.

Figure 2.1. How the Aircraft Sustainability Model Calculates Readiness Spares Package Composition

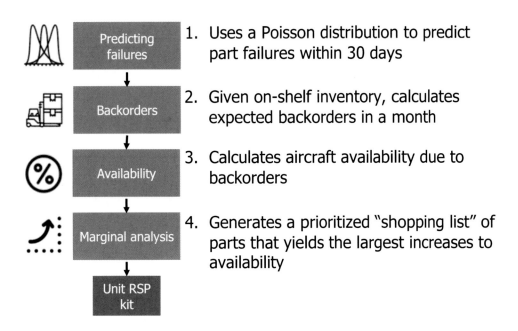

1. Uses a Poisson distribution to predict part failures within 30 days

2. Given on-shelf inventory, calculates expected backorders in a month

3. Calculates aircraft availability due to backorders

4. Generates a prioritized "shopping list" of parts that yields the largest increases to availability

ASM predicts part failures (and thus demand for spare parts) for a given base within a 30-day period. Using this prediction and the amount of on-shelf inventory, ASM estimates the shortfall (number of backorders) in parts. Each backordered part, across all bases, results in not-mission-capable aircraft and decreases fleet-wide availability. Finally, ASM performs marginal analysis by iteratively identifying the least expensive spare part that yields the greatest increase to fleet-wide availability. The output is a shopping list of spare parts that decisionmakers can use to calculate RSP compositions. With marginal analysis, ASM helps decisionmakers answer two kinds of questions: (1) What availability can be achieved with a given budget and (2) what is the cost to achieve this target availability?

Failure analysis is the core of ASM's functionality and the foundation for the entire RSP predictive maintenance analysis. ASM predicts part failures solely on the basis of the anticipated flying hours for contingency operations, as dictated by the War and Mobilization Plan (WMP). ASM assumes that part failures are characterized by a stationary Poisson distribution driven by the mean hourly demand. This demand, in addition to on-shelf base inventory, is used to calculate the number of expected backorders, which powers the subsequent availability and marginal analysis calculations.[6] As a result, the Poisson distribution assumption is crucial to ASM's optimal RSP composition calculation.

---

[6] For a detailed description and derivation of these calculations, see F. Michael Slay, Tovey C. Bachman, Robert C. Kline, T. J. O'Malley, Frank L. Eichorn, and Randall M. King, *Optimizing Spares Support: The Aircraft Sustainability Model*, AF501MR1, Logistics Management Institute, October 1996.

Assessment of Readiness Spares Package Modeling Assumptions

ASM makes several modeling assumptions to calculate RSPs. The first assumption is that part failures can be modeled as a stationary Poisson process. The second assumption is that part failures are estimated solely on the basis of flying hours. The third assumption is that 30 days is sufficient for supply lines to be reestablished. In this section, we assess the validity of these assumptions to identify areas where AI can make improvements.

The Poisson Distribution

The current approach to failure analysis is to generate predictions by sampling a stationary Poisson distribution. To generate this Poisson distribution, a per-hour failure rate, known as the total organizational and intermediate maintenance demand rate (TOIMDR), is multiplied by the number of anticipated flying hours in a given 30-day period. TOIMDR is also known as the *demand rate*.[7] Although ASM supports both Poisson and negative binomial probability distributions to model part failures, negative binomial probability distributions are not currently used.

The Poisson distribution is useful to predict discrete outputs (e.g., number of events) given a mean rate, usually over a unit of time. The probability of x events happening is expressed as follows:

$$P(x; \mu) = \frac{e^{-\mu} \mu^x}{x!}$$

where x is a discrete number and μ is the mean rate of the event occurring. For failure analysis, μ is typically expressed as a failure rate per flying hour, λ, multiplied by flying hours: $\mu = \lambda * FH$.

Previous research and our interviews show us that part failures are not Poisson-distributed with respect to flying hours (FH).[8] For example, according to USAF logistics subject-matter experts, some part failures are better characterized by the number of sorties flown rather than by flying hours (e.g., landing gears).[9] We attempted to empirically test this characterization using the parts failure data, but there were not enough data. Instead, we needed to calculate the number of flying hours each part experienced before failure. The parts failure data did not contain enough repeat failures across serial numbers to provide a temporal duration between failures. The vehicle configuration data provide

---

[7] Stephen D. Gray, *Mitigating Growth Cost for Mobility Readiness Spares Packages*, thesis, Air Force Institute of Technology, March 2004.

[8] Slay et al., 1996; Patrick Mills, Sarah A. Nowak, Peter Buryk, John G. Drew, Christopher Guo, and Raffaele Vardavas, *Increasing Cost-Effective Readiness for the U.S. Air Force by Reducing Supply Chain Variance: Technical Analysis of Flying Hour Program Variance*, RAND Corporation, RR-2118-AF, 2018.

[9] Craig C. Sherbrooke, *Using Sorties vs. Flying Hours to Predict Aircraft Spares Demand*, AF501LN1, Logistics Management Institute, April 1997.

circumstantial evidence that failures are not Poisson-distributed, but we are not certain what types of failures these data encompassed.[10]

Estimating Failure Rates

There is a lack of data to inform the RSP calculation process, which greatly challenges failure analysis. RSPs are designed to predict part failures during contingency sorties. However, many subject-matter experts told us that the USAF has not flown many contingency operations in recent decades and that data are scarce. Each USAF aircraft requires an RSP, which contains dozens or hundreds of spare parts. There are not enough data to derive failure trends (and to calculate the TOIMDR parameter) for every part. Even with peacetime data, our A-10C query from the Logistics, Installations, and Mission Support–Enterprise View (LIMS-EV) system for the 110 relevant RSP parts revealed 33 parts that did not experience any failures.[11]

Furthermore, the guidance for anticipated contingency flying hours is currently outdated. RSPs derive flying hours on the basis of the WMP, but at of the time of this writing, the last WMP was published in 2011. AFSC subject-matter experts acknowledge that RSPs are typically designed for operations that are not actually flown.[12] A previous RAND report that presented an assessment of the performance of spares prediction performance concluded that

> Operations Desert Shield and Desert Storm were characterized by unanticipated levels of demand for U.S. Air Force (USAF) fighter logistics materials and services— sometimes high, sometimes low, but seldom what was predicted during peacetime planning. Peacetime predictions about the required kinds, quantities, and locations of critical logistics resources were frequently wrong—often substantially.[13]

The report attributed logistical successes in Desert Storm mostly to the eventual formation of Desert Express, a daily logistics flight that enabled units to request spares and receive them in two days. In lieu of contingency data and recent flying hour guidance, the only course of action appears to be to derive demand rates from peacetime failures and continuously update the failure rates as parts fail, especially during contingencies.

It is important to highlight that the TOIMDRs for RSPs appear to be static and do not update over time. Our interviews with AFSC analysts informed us that the USAF does not have a policy to update RSP TOIMDR parameters using recent empirical data (e.g., using a moving average). It is unclear how the TOIMDR is currently derived given the rarity of certain part failures and the absence

---

[10] We tested the vehicle configuration data, which contain temporal data between failures, but recall that these data could not be matched to the parts failure data. Although we were not certain what types of maintenance these data encompassed, we tested these data in an exploratory analysis. Using the Kolmogorov-Smirnov (KS) test on flying hours (using $p < 0.05$ cutoffs), we identified that only 84 percent of parts were not Poisson-distributed. We tested other factors, but they were not Poisson-distributed either (e.g., sorties to failure was not Poisson-distributed in 95 percent of parts; days to failure was not Poisson-distributed in 97.5 percent of parts).

[11] Note that we did not find a suitable metric to distinguish between contingency and peacetime sorties within the LIMS-EV data. We assume that most of the failure data that we collected are associated with peacetime flying.

[12] See also Blazer, 2011.

[13] Raymond A. Pyles and Hyman L. Shulman, *United States Air Force Fighter Support in Operation Desert Storm*, RAND Corporation, MR-468-AF, 1995, pp. xi–xii.

of contingency data. We identified a source who explained how to calculate the TOIMDR for unobserved rare failures, which suggests that some values might not be derived from empirical data.[14] This makes it even more critical that the TOIMDR is updated via data feedback, even during peacetime.

To illustrate this point, we compare the part failure data against the A-10C TOIMDR parameters within ASM. The time window for this analysis encompasses September 2007 to June 2022. For each part, we calculated the average monthly failure rate. We calculate predicted monthly demand as follows:[15]

$$\frac{FH_{total}}{elapsedMonths} * TOIMDR * QPA * AP,$$

from which we first calculate the 30-day average flying hours in the 15-year period, multiply by the TOIMDR parameter, multiply by quantity per application (QPA), referring to the number of parts required per aircraft, and then multiply by the application percentage (AP), referring to the percentage of the fleet with this part. Figure 2.2 shows a scatterplot of predicted monthly failures (y-axis) against observed average monthly failures (x-axis). The red dashed line represents $y = x$, which indicates that a prediction aligns closely with observed failures.

---

[14] Timothy J. Sakulich and George Zeck, *Computation of ECM War Reserve Materiel Spare Requirements*, Air Force Logistics Command, November 1987.

[15] Slay et al., 1996; Gray, 2004.

Figure 2.2. Comparison of Empirical Failure Rates to the Aircraft Sustainability Model Failure Rate Parameters

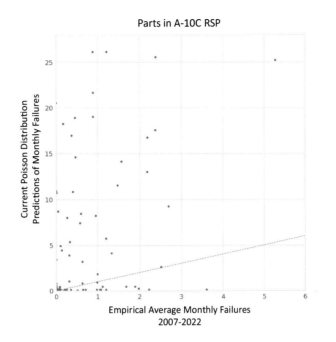

NOTE: The scatterplot depicts the average monthly failures of various A-10C RSP parts. Poisson parameters (y-axis) are presented across empirical failures (x-axis). The red dotted line, representing *y = x*, is provided for reference.

Figure 2.2 shows that the A-10C TOIMDR parameters within ASM do not appear to correlate with empirical peacetime values. It is worth noting that the parameter is currently designed to overpredict failures to minimize the risk of units running out of spares. According to AFSC subject-matter experts, units that receive extra spares might not be incentivized to complain or provide feedback; having extra spares is beneficial because it keeps unit readiness metrics high. Note that it is difficult to directly compare the TOIMDR against empirical rates because of the assumption that failure rates are solely a function of flying hours. Such a comparison could be possible with a flying hours-between-failures database, but we were unable to confidently derive such data for this project.[16]

Figure 2.2 illustrates the inherent difficulty of predicting part failures, especially by extrapolating peacetime flying data. One of the most straightforward policy changes would be to update the TOIMDR on a moving basis to enable logisticians to react to changing (or unknown) demand.[17]

30-Day Supply Chain

Unpublished research from Air Force Materiel Command (AFMC) analyzed depot repair times and depot-hub-base shipment times and concluded that 30 days might not be sufficient. Desert

---

[16] See the "Vehicle Configuration Database" section in Appendix A.

[17] This sentiment is echoed in Pyles and Shulman (1995, p. xviii), which introduces the concept of "lean logistics," the idea that if the number of spare parts is wrong anyway, at least stockpiles of extraneous parts should be avoided. During Desert Storm, WRSK parts were all deemed high priority, and overpredicted parts clogged up ports.

Express took longer than 30 days to be established.[18] The current RSP process also assumes that all individual bases are the same with respect to failure rates, base repair capabilities, and depot-to-base shipment times.[19] Focusing on just the shipment time assumption, AFMC research revealed that shipment time is quite long and highly variable, especially during wartime. The 30-day assumption, as well as constant shipping times, could be weak assumptions in 2022. However, these weaknesses could be balanced by the model's tendency to overpredict.

Areas to Explore for Improvements by Artificial Intelligence

ASM is currently used to calculate RSPs, and it tackles a highly complex problem. Managing failure analysis across myriad parts across different aircraft, multiple bases, and depots is a difficult logistics and operations research problem that is not currently suited for AI. However, there could be potential for improvement in the narrow component of failure analysis. In the previous assessment, we identified the challenges of failure analysis, especially by extrapolating peacetime flying data. In the absence of contingency data, the best option is to learn from peacetime data and quickly update that data as time goes on.

In Chapter 3, we explore what happens when we update the Poisson distribution to match empirical failure rates and compare this performance against that of a trained AI algorithm in terms of prediction performance and cost.

---

[18] Pyles and Shulman, 1995.

[19] According to Slay et al., 1996. The AFSC data, dated June 2002, indicate that current processes still use these assumptions.

Assessing the Potential for Artificial Intelligence

Focusing on just the failure analysis aspect of RSP calculations, this chapter is focused on addressing two questions: How well does the Poisson distribution predict part failures, and how well can AI predict part failures? Through this exploration, we assess the feasibility of AI and its limitations for this predictive maintenance application.

Developing Performance Metrics

Developing performance metrics for prediction performance is difficult given the rare event nature of part failures. The 2020 Department of Defense *Supply Chain Metrics Guide* defines forecast accuracy as follows:[20]

$$Accuracy = 1 - \frac{\Sigma \left(|y - \hat{y}| * value \right)}{\Sigma \left(y * value \right)},$$

where y is the actual demand and $\hat{y}$ is the predicted demand. This metric is based on the mean average percent error (MAPE) family of metrics. We will use MAPE to simplify calculations and avoid using spares cost to bias forecast accuracy, thus obtaining accuracy with respect to actual demand volume. MAPE is defined as follows:

$$MAPE = \frac{1}{N} \frac{\Sigma |y - \hat{y}|}{\Sigma y}.$$

These metrics are very similar in concept, but, as we will see, they are poor metrics with respect to assessing RSP performance.

The rare event nature of many RSP National Item Identification Number (NIIN) failures renders MAPE-based metrics a poor choice. To illustrate this, we developed a zero-prediction model ($\hat{y} = 0$, always). The MAPE was 1.53 percent, averaged across all A-10C NIINs (0 percent indicates a perfect model).[21] For comparison, our linear regression model in Figure 3.4 scored a 5.1 percent MAPE, while the current Poisson distribution scored 119 percent. As a result, we decided not to use MAPE as a performance metric.

---

[20] U.S. Department of Defense, *Supply Chain Metrics Guide*, 2nd ed., 2020.

[21] Note that there are 110 unique parts in the A-10C RSP. We were only able to locate failure data for 77 of those parts, implying that 33 parts have not yet experienced a failure since 2007. We excluded those 33 parts from our analysis because there is no historical data with which to predict failures.

From our conversations with AFSC subject-matter experts, we learned that RSPs are evaluated on the basis of forecast accuracy and cost. Rather than developing a single metric, we opted to calculate performance across the following metrics:

- average monthly overprediction (For months when we overpredict, how much do we overpredict on average?)
- average monthly underprediction (For months when we underpredict, how much do we underpredict on average?)
- average cost of monthly overpredictions.

During the course of the research, we identified that it was very difficult to exactly predict monthly demand; predictions were almost always over or under actual monthly demand. We used two metrics, average overprediction and average underprediction, to clearly show prediction performance and any potential biases. Furthermore, to illustrate the extraneous implementation cost of various algorithms, we calculated the cost of overpredictions. We ignored the cost of underpredictions because it represents the cost that should have been spent.

A potential drawback of this metric is that it does not penalize against underprediction frequency. We addressed this shortcoming by tuning our model toward overpredicting at the end of the chapter. Another drawback of this metric is the lack of an aircraft availability calculation. However, we were not provided access to ASM during this project and did not have sufficient data to compute A-10C availability.

Performance of an Updated Empirical Poisson Distribution

To illustrate these metrics, we assessed the failure analysis performance of two Poisson distributions. To compare performance, we completed a retrospective analysis on parts failure data from **September 2007 to June 2022**. We used data from September 2007 to June 2017 as a training set and the remaining five years of data, June 2017 to June 2022, as the validation set. Performance across this five-year validation period is shown in all results in this chapter, including an assessment of the Poisson distribution, to provide a like-for-like comparison.

For each A-10C RSP part, we predicted demand for the five-year period by sampling the Poisson distribution as informed by the current ASM TOIMDR parameter. (We used the equation provided in Chapter 2 to derive our Poisson mean.) We call this the "current Poisson distribution." We compared this performance of the Poisson distribution set with the empirical monthly failure rate for each RSP part.[22] We call this the "updated Poisson distribution." Given the stochastic nature of predictions, we drew 10,000 monthly samples for this five-year period and calculated metrics. Figure 3.1 illustrates the average overprediction and underprediction performance between the two Poisson distributions.

---

[22] Using the parts failure data (September 2007 to June 2022), we calculated the empirical monthly failure rate and set the Poisson distribution mean to this value. These are the same values as those shown on the x-axis of Figure 3.1. Note that this is "cheating" in a traditional machine-learning approach because we are using empirical values derived partially from the testing data, which we deemed as June 2017 to June 2022. The purpose of this section is to illustrate the upper limit of predictive performance.

Figure 3.1. Updated Poisson Monthly Performance for the A-10C Readiness Spares Package Kit

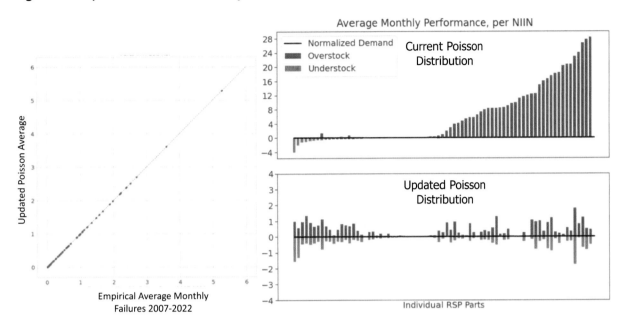

NOTE: Figure 3.1 consists of three parts. The chart on the left-hand side (scatterplot) depicts the performance of the predictive Poisson algorithm (y-axis) tuned to empirical average monthly failures (x-axis). A $y = x$ line (dotted red line) is shown. The chart on the top right-hand side shows the per part performance of the current Poisson distribution. Average monthly overprediction is shown as a positive blue bar (overstock), and average monthly underprediction is shown as a negative orange bar (understock) across a five-year period (June 2017–June 2022). The x-axis is an unlabeled categorical axis consisting of the parts contained in the A-10C RSP kit. The chart on the bottom right-hand side depicts the performance of the updated Poisson distribution. Each blue and orange pair along the x-axis represents a different spare part, and the parts between the top and bottom subplots are aligned.

In Figure 3.1, each positive blue bar and negative orange bar in the two graphs on the right-hand side represents the respective average monthly overprediction and underprediction performance for a unique spare part. Parts are sorted relative to the current Poisson distribution's performance and are aligned between the subplots. For example, an examination of the left portion of the subplots shows that the current Poisson distribution (the graph in the upper right-hand corner), on average, underpredicts by 4 parts every month. The updated Poisson distribution (the graph in the lower right-hand corner) does better: Each month, it tends to overpredict by 1 part or underpredict by 1.5 parts. As we mentioned in Chapter 2, the current Poisson distribution is tuned to overpredict parts. For half of the RSP parts, it overpredicts by 8 to 28 parts each month and never underpredicts. In contrast, the updated Poisson distribution understocks more (1-2 parts each month) but keeps extraneous spares at a minimum (1-2 parts each month). On average, the current Poisson distribution overstocks $31 million worth of parts each month, and the updated Poisson distribution overstocks $1.9 million worth of parts.

These results show the predictive performance of using the Poisson distribution if it is updated to reflect data trends. Setting the TOIMDR to empirical, real-world values (for example, calculating a 12-month moving average) is a cheap and simple policy to achieve better predictions. Although this approach is still limited to deriving wartime demand from peacetime flying, it is better than the status quo, which appears to be rooted in no data at all. Furthermore, a faster update cycle (e.g., a three-month moving average) during contingencies could help the USAF respond faster to demand signals and improve prediction performance.

Performance of Machine-Learning Algorithms

Developing Neural Networks

Figure 3.2 shows the testing and training scheme for neural networks. As shown, we used data from a ten-year period as the training set and data from the remaining five years as a test set. We used a six-month sliding window to update the neural networks and to predict the next month's demand.

Figure 3.2. Artificial Intelligence Training and Testing Scheme

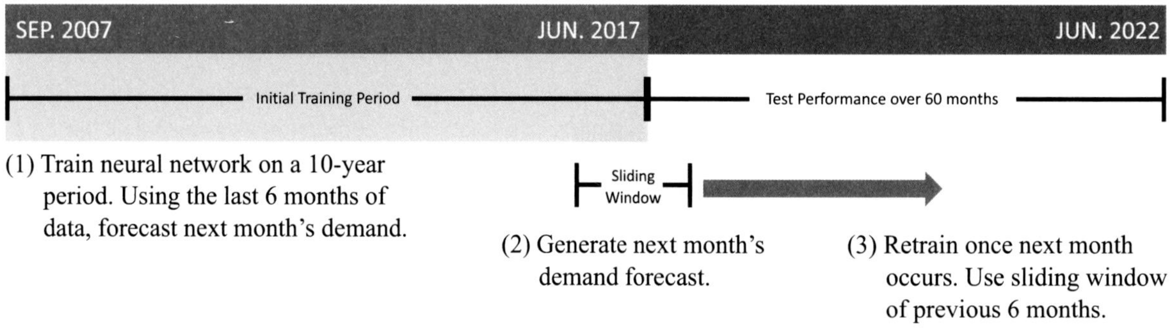

SEP. 2007	JUN. 2017	JUN. 2022
Initial Training Period	Test Performance over 60 months	

(1) Train neural network on a 10-year period. Using the last 6 months of data, forecast next month's demand.

Sliding Window

(2) Generate next month's demand forecast.

(3) Retrain once next month occurs. Use sliding window of previous 6 months.

The parts failure data from LIMS-EV encompass about 15 years, and we used the last five years as the test set. Given the propensity for data to be outdated, we opted for a six-month sliding window to continuously update the model and generate new predictions.[23] We used the previous six months of two predictors, flying hours and sortie numbers, to anticipate failure rates for the subsequent month. Although other variables from our LIMS-EV queries could serve as potential predictors of failure, we were unable to clean and join them in time for this analysis. However, exploratory analysis on using days to failure as an additional predictor is available in Appendix B. We use the aforementioned average performance metrics to assess the neural networks across the parts within the A-10C RSP kit and the parts failure data. We tried simple linear regression, but it was unsatisfactory.[24]

Choosing the neural network architecture required a fair amount of trial and error. Preliminary testing revealed that using a long short-term memory (LSTM) architecture seemed to outperform a purely linear, fully connected network. Using LSTM, we tested two types of neural network architectures. The architectures are summarized in Figure 3.3.

---

[23] For example, to predict the parts for July 2017, we used data from the previous six months (January 2017 to June 2017). After July 2017, we updated the model with the new month and used February 2017 to July 2017 to predict parts for August 2017.

[24] Our linear regression model skewed heavily toward underpredicting because it predicted near-zero (outputs between 0 and 1) failures per month for most parts.

Figure 3.3. Neural Network Architectures Evaluated

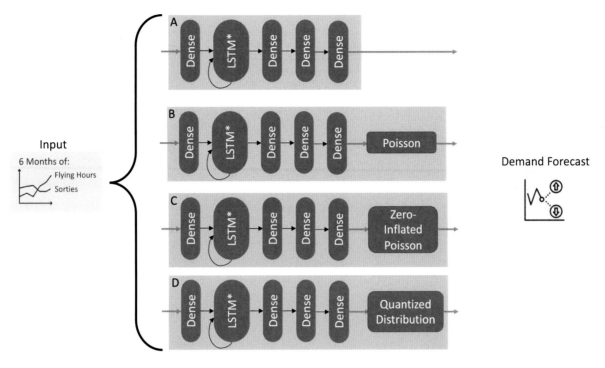

NOTE: We tested four neural network architectures (depicted in networks A through D). Each architecture was fed the same inputs: six months of A-10C flying hours and the number of sorties. All networks involve LSTM to learn temporal dynamics. Network A directly yields a prediction (that must be rounded). Networks B, C, and D output probability distributions that must be sampled to yield a prediction. Predictive performance across these networks is very similar, and for simplicity, we only moved forward with network A.

For the first type of neural network architecture (see network A in Figure 3.3), we treated the problem as pure regression: directly output the prediction with a rectifying unit (a fully connected layer of size 1 with negative values truncated to 0 because it is nonsensical to predict negative demand). For the second type (see networks B, C, and D in Figure 3.3), we treated the problem as fitting a nonstationary probability distribution: We fed neural network outputs into probability distributions, from which we sampled to obtain predictions. We tested the Poisson, zero-inflated Poisson, and quantized distributions.

Interestingly, the probability distribution–based architectures did not perform significantly differently from the direct prediction architecture (in most cases, they were slightly worse). For the rest of Chapter 3, we focus on the direct prediction network (depicted in Figure 3.3 as network A). We learned from our conversations with AFSC subject-matter experts that the Logistics Management Institute has tested many probability distributions over the years and has more expertise in this area.

Performance of Linear Regression

Prior to trying any neural network, it is a good idea to benchmark the performance of linear regression. Furthermore, ESCAPE, which replaced the D200A system (which predicted peacetime operating spares for the USAF), uses linear regression as one of its prediction engines.[25] Using the sliding six-month technique described above, Figure 3.4 shows the linear regression results.

Figure 3.4. Performance of a Linear Regression Model to Predict Failure Rates

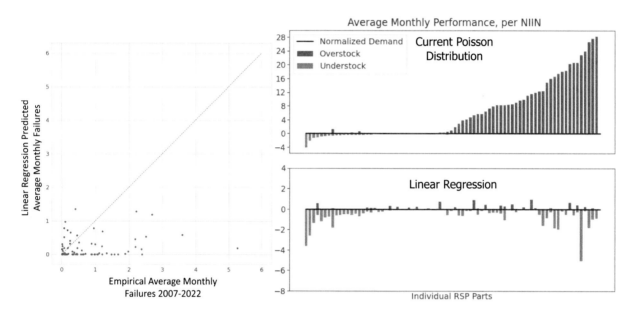

NOTE: Figure 3.4 consists of three parts in the same format as Figure 3.1. It depicts the predictive performance of a linear regression across a five-year period (June 2017 to June 2022). The chart on the left-hand side shows a scatterplot of predicted versus empirical average monthly failure rates. The charts on the right-hand side show the average monthly overprediction and underprediction performance (lower plot) compared with the current Poisson distribution (upper plot).

Linear regression performs poorly in this case because it tends to predict between 0 and 2 parts, regardless of empirical failure rates. Although this algorithm overbuys $410,000 worth of parts each month, we see high levels of underprediction (understocking spares). The algorithm performs worse for every single part when compared with the current Poisson distribution and, therefore, should not be considered.

Performance of the Long Short-Term Memory Regression Neural Network

Figure 3.5 shows the results for neural network A depicted in Figure 3.3. Its overprediction and underprediction performance is very similar to the empirical Poisson distribution (shown in Figure 3.1). The scatterplot shows that the neural network tends to overpredict. For most parts, the neural network gets the prediction to within ± 2 parts each month. Each month, the neural network overbuys by about $1.1 million worth of parts.

---

[25] ESCAPE uses linear regression, Poisson distributions, and moving averages to generate demand predictions of peacetime operating spares. See Lee R. Russell, *A Feasibility Analysis on the Air Force Employment of ESCAPE Supply Chain Management Program*, Air Force Institute of Technology, June 2020.

Figure 3.5. Performance of a Regression Neural Network with Long Short-Term Memory to Predict Failure Rates

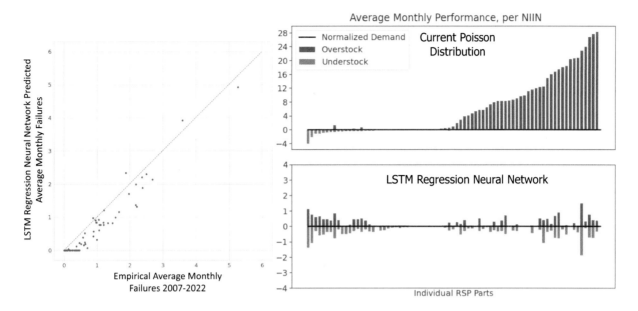

NOTE: Figure 3.5 consists of three parts in the same format as Figure 3.1. It depicts the predictive performance of a neural network (network A in Figure 3.3) across a five-year period (June 2017 to June 2022). The chart on the left-hand side shows a scatterplot of predicted versus empirical average monthly failure rates. The charts on the right-hand side show the average monthly overprediction and underprediction performance (lower plot) compared with the current Poisson distribution (upper plot).

Note that within the scatterplot, there is a cluster of points where the neural network constantly predicts zero. These points represent a region of rare part failures for which there are insufficient data to properly train the neural network to predict failures; as a result, the network makes predictions of zero for all these parts.

Performance of the Long Short-Term Memory Regression Neural Network with Asymmetrical Cost

In the realm of predictive maintenance, and for RSPs specifically, underprediction is generally worse than overprediction. Overprediction (budget permitting) is generally better, especially if the assumption of a 30-day return to normal supply lines is no longer trustworthy. To demonstrate this, we retrained the neural network with an asymmetrical cost function to heavily penalize underpredicting as follows:

$$\varepsilon = \hat{y} - y$$

$$L = \varepsilon^2 (\text{sign}(\varepsilon) + 0.75)^2,$$

where we define error as prediction minus truth (underpredictions are negative).

Figure 3.6 shows the performance for this network. Both the scatterplot and bar graph show that the neural network now prefers to overpredict each month. There are barely any understocked parts, and overpredictions average about 4–5 parts each month. This algorithm overbuys by about $5.9 million worth of parts each month, which is well under the $31 million spent using the current Poisson distribution.

Figure 3.6. Performance of an Adjusted Regression Neural Network with Long Short-Term Memory to Predict Failure Rates

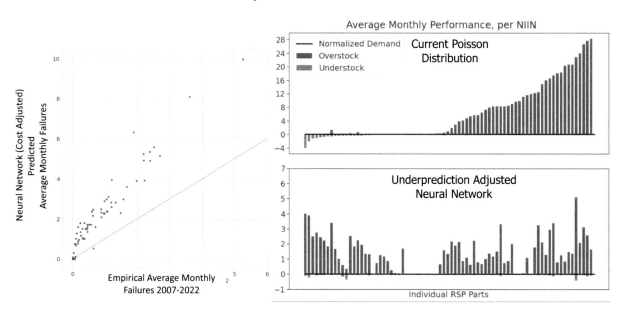

NOTE: Figure 3.6 consists of three parts in the same format as Figure 3.1. It depicts the predictive performance of a modified neural network (network A in Figure 3.3) across a five-year period (June 2017 to June 2022). The network has been adjusted to penalize underpredictions during training, unlike the network referenced in Figure 3.5. The chart on the left-hand side shows a scatterplot of predicted versus empirical average monthly failure rates. The charts on the right-hand side show the average monthly overprediction and underprediction performance (lower plot) compared with the current Poisson distribution (upper plot).

Note that there is still a small cluster of points on the bottom left of the scatterplot that indicates that the network is unable to properly predict rare part failures. Although the asymmetrical cost function helped greatly, there are still a handful of parts for which the neural network predicts zero failures.

Summary

In this chapter, we explored the potential for AI to improve the RSP process. Specifically, we tested the performance of a neural network and showed that it can improve failure analysis in many aspects. The neural network can make better predictions (less understocking of parts) and do it more cheaply (less overstocking). However, our neural network performs similarly to an empirically based Poisson distribution. Even though the observed failure rates do not conform to a Poisson process, the empirical Poisson distribution performs very well and is much simpler to implement.

One of the most challenging aspects of creating RSPs is that there are not enough contingency data. AI cannot solve this problem, but it can help indirectly. Neural networks in general tend to require constant retraining and monitoring; this requirement serves as a forcing function to detect any changes in data. Although setting the TOIMDR to an empirical moving average is simpler, this is likely not done currently and is a potential cause for the poor distribution performance of the current Poisson. Responding to changes dynamically was a critical part of Operation Desert Storm and will likely be important in future conflicts, as USAF logisticians react to new, never-before-seen demand signals.

Another limitation of AI is that it tends to poorly predict rare events. We can see in the scatterplots that our neural network tends to predict 0 for parts that rarely experience (but still have non-zero) failures. A stationary Poisson might be the best solution in this case because overpredicting is the safer option. We explore a different approach to this problem in Appendix B using a neural network to model time to failure; however, this exploratory analysis was conducted on a dataset that we are not confident wholly represents part failures.

Finally, it is worth highlighting that all the failure analysis explored in this chapter is limited to a single-depot, single-base assumption. Despite all of the modeling assumptions, ASM tackles a vastly more difficult and complex problem that involves predicting demands from multiple bases. Most of this process is better suited as operations research and should be scoped outside AI territory. From a pure prediction performance standpoint, AI might be slightly better, but this performance should be considered on a part-by-part basis. For example, the USAF can save money on RSP kits by leveraging AI to help with the selection of parts that the current Poisson distribution overpredicts monthly by 10+ parts.

Chapter 4

Challenges in Collecting and Preparing Maintenance Data for Artificial Intelligence

In this chapter, we describe in detail how we derived the empirical part failure data required by our analysis. As discussed in Chapter 1, we limited our analysis to a single aircraft series: the A-10C. Deriving the appropriate search queries and data links within the USAF maintenance data systems is a complex process. The AFSC compiled RSP data for several aircraft series, one of which was the A-10C. We describe the process that we used to obtain historical part failures, flying hours, and cost data for the A-10C. Development of this process took considerable time, and resource limitations narrowed down our analysis to this single aircraft series. Although we have not exhaustively tested this process across other aircraft series, we believe that this process is generalizable.

Figure 4.1 summarizes our overall data derivation process to obtain parts failure data from the USAF logistics database. Within LIMS-EV, the access portal to the data, a series of data pulls is required. The IMDS with Current Records database provides a dictionary to convert RSP parts into part numbers. These part numbers can be referenced in the Aerospace Veh Configuration database to obtain the WUCs that correspond to the parts of interest. We filtered down these codes to maintenance actions that pertain to part failures. Using the filtered code list, we searched the

Figure 4.1. Deriving Empirical Part Failures from LIMS-EV Data

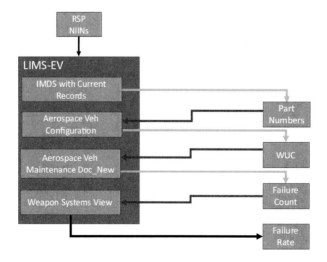

NOTE: IMDS = integrated maintenance data system; Veh = vehicle; WUC = work unit code.

Aerospace Veh Maintenance Doc_New database to find when a relevant maintenance action occurred for every A-10C airframe. Finally, we parsed the Weapon Systems View database to obtain the daily number of sorties and flying hours that each A-10C experienced. This final step provided the critical link between failures as a function of airframe usage. An in-depth description of this methodology is provided in Appendix A.

The complexity of this process highlights a major USAF limitation to using AI. The USAF locks its maintenance data behind a complex and manually labor-intensive web portal. Although LIMS-EV was designed with other requirements in mind, the system's current state hampers automation and AI. To the best of our knowledge, LIMS-EV does not offer easy ways to automatically pull data. Instead, analysts are required to manually pull data via a mixture of pseudocode and drop-down menus. We required multiple consultations with experts on the system to learn how to navigate the portal. Rather than solving problems, LIMS-EV burdens analysts with navigating its obscure procedures. This difficulty could be another reason why RSPs are not retrospectively validated and why obtaining feedback on kit composition is difficult.

Enabling an RSP data view within LIMS-EV (i.e., saving a data processing formula within the system to automatically generate relevant parts failure data) would greatly enhance this process. Although LIMS-EV allows a user to enter code to process data, such code is limited to single database queries. These singular databases appear to be organized to address specific maintenance needs, but most logistics analyses require data joins, which the system cannot handle. As a result, analysts must pull data and perform processing offline, which generates static intermediary files that obfuscate data lineages and frustrate the timely data processing that AI systems need.

Chapter 5

Summary of Findings and Recommendations

In this report, we considered how AI could be used to improve the failure analysis process for RSPs. The test case of A-10C data demonstrated that AI, specifically neural networks, can offer value in this area. The primary limitations of AI use concern data: a dearth of wartime flying data requires extrapolation using historical peacetime flying data, and the USAF lacks a data operations pipeline to easily pull the historical data on which AI models can be trained. We summarize these findings and our recommendations below.

Findings

AI can improve failure analysis for RSPs on a case-by-case basis. Compared with the static Poisson process that the USAF currently uses, we show that AI can generate better predictions and save money. Specifically, in our narrowly scoped analysis, the AI predictions would cost $25.1 million per month less than the overpredictions of the Poisson process. Although we only showed this for a single platform (A-10C), the results are likely generalizable because our statistical tests showed that part failures are not quite governed by the Poisson process. However, we did not consider the larger issue of allocation from depots to bases. Current Poisson distributions do not seem to be rooted in empirical data; we demonstrated that updating these distributions with data can achieve an upper limit of performance that is close to the AI predictions. Comparisons of performance reveal regimes in which AI does better (parts with more frequent failures) and in which AI does worse (parts with rare failures).

A complex and labor-intensive data operations pipeline to USAF maintenance databases is necessary before any AI application can occur. Pulling LIMS-EV data is a manual process that involves scripting, drop-down lists, and nested menus. It is practical only for proof-of-concept models of the kinds described in this research. Moreover, considerable data cleaning is necessary to unlock historical data (e.g., linking variants prior to platform upgrades) and other potential predictors of failure. It might be unrealistic to conduct this analysis on multiple platforms by attempting to make these LIMS-EV data pulls manually. Automation might be necessary for these data pulls *before* AI can be applied.

AI cannot alleviate the scarcity of wartime data. Additional assumptions and policy considerations will be needed to account for this scarcity. As mentioned, one of the main limitations for the application of AI in this use case is its inability to estimate truly rare events. Certain events in war could be considered rare because of their unpredictable nature. As a result, different approaches to modeling AI might be required to deal with these changing circumstances. However, a regular retraining and updating policy, which is possible with an AI model, can ensure adaptability during war.

Recommendations for Air Force Materiel Command

Work with USAF Logistics (A4) to build a data operations pipeline to conduct retrospective analysis of aircraft maintenance and RSP efficiency. Aircraft maintenance programs and databases function effectively for the purposes for which they were designed, but they were not designed for retrospective analysis or to train AI models. Unless the data can be properly conditioned and pulled for this analysis, none of the following recommendations can be implemented.

Experiment with AI to improve failure analysis for RSPs. Extend the proof-of-concept models to all aircraft. This extension will likely have to be done on a part-by-part, platform-by-platform basis. Automated or partially automated data extraction will likely be necessary if AI is used to conduct these analyses. For RSP parts with hard-to-predict rare failures, we can modify the AI model's cost function to prefer overpredictions or rely on overpredictions via a Poisson distribution or the problem can be modeled as survival analysis (predict time to failure).

Limit AI to failure analysis within the RSP process. The ASM software tackles a large and complex operations research problem of selecting which parts to send from which depot to which base. Current AI capabilities are data hungry and better suited to solving narrowly scoped problems. Splitting parts failures across multiple depots and bases will fragment the data too much for algorithms to learn anything useful.

In-Depth Methodology for Deriving Parts Failure Data from LIMS-EV and Other Supporting Information

Databases

RSPs consist of a supplement of spare line-replaceable units (LRUs) for aircraft systems that deploy with aircraft and units for 30-day periods during war. These supplements are sent in addition to the usual peacetime operating stock that is available during peacetime operations.

The LRUs on the aircraft are inspected and, under certain conditions, can be replaced with items from both the RSP and/or the peacetime operating stock. We used the LRU data to find ways to leverage AI and machine learning to build better RSPs that improve spare part availability and use. This analysis of historical LRU use data could enable the USAF to identify replacement rate trends of RSP items.

The methodology uses RSP data provided by the AFSC's LIMS-EV data. In this appendix, we document our use of LIMS-EV, describe the steps taken to pull the appropriate data, and discuss the processing and cleaning steps taken prior to the analysis presented in the report.

The LIMS-EV System

LIMS-EV is the interactive web tool used to access the Air Force Reliability and Maintainability Information System. LIMS-EV has a data access application called Business Objects Web Intelligence, within which many databases can be accessed as data sources to extract useful information from a wide variety of results via logical operators and filtering. Depending on the database, the LIMS-EV online tool provides an interface to filter across any set of parameters. Despite the availability of a scripting language to allow data filtering, the overall process is labor-intensive and requires a mixture of scripts and drop-down selection menus.

Databases that LIMS-EV can access include IMDS with Current Records, which provides weekly updates of D043 data (a stock number database); Aerospace Veh Configuration, which provides updated near real-time approved and actual aircraft equipment configuration data; and Aerospace Veh Maintenance Doc_New, which provides maintenance record data, also updated near real time. During data pulls, we requested a time range of June 2007 to June 2022 to encompass the service start day of the A-10C aircraft to the year this report was written.

Readiness Spares Package File

An example RSP data file was provided by the AFSC. Within the example RSP data file, one of three mission design series (MDS) is associated with a table containing NIINs in a given year. These tables also contain Federal Supply Classification codes, demand per operating hour values, authorized quantities, and cost per part. Each MDS file has two sheets: one containing demand history and the other containing costs and other parameters, such as the TOIMDR. The demand history varies from fiscal year 2014 to fiscal year 2023, and each part has a respective number of flying hours associated with it until it failed. Because our previous analysis was focused on the A-10C and because of the LIMS-EV data download limitations, we used only the A-10C MDS from these data.

Methodology

Beginning with an RSP listing for a given MDS provided by the AFSC, the MDS is linked to a set of NIINs within the RSP listing file table. The NIINs in this table can then be individually looked up within the LIMS-EV IMDS with the Current Records database in order to link each MDS/NIIN combination to its part number. A given MDS/NIIN combination will often cross-reference to multiple part numbers that represent the same end item.

Once the part numbers are linked to their respective NIINs in the RSP table for a given MDS, the Aerospace Veh Configuration database, another source within LIMS-EV, can be used to cross-reference the part numbers to corresponding WUCs in the given MDS. A given part number will often cross-reference to multiple WUCs.

After the WUCs have been linked to their respective NIINs in the RSP table for a given MDS, the Aerospace Veh Maintenance Doc_New database, another source within LIMS-EV, can be used to filter maintenance records for inherent failures, induced failures, and no defect actions.

Defining Part Failure

Technical Order (TO) 00-20-2 defines *total failure* as "TOTAL FAILURES = INHERENT FAILURES + INDUCED FAILURES + NO DEFECT ACTIONS."[26]

From this definition, the three datasets—inherent failure, induced failure, and no defect actions—can be joined to form a single dataset that consists of total part failures. TO 00-20-2 defines *inherent failure* as "an actual failure of an item," *induced failure* as "the failure of an item . . . caused by an outside influence," and *no defect* as "no actual failure."[27]

Although it might seem odd to include no defect as part of total failures, it makes sense given the USAF's spares inventory policy.[28] When a part is suspected to have failed, the worker removes this part and orders a replacement part, triggering demand. The removed part is later inspected at the base to determine whether it can be repaired or not. Regardless of the inspection outcome (e.g., no defect),

---

[26] TO 00-20-2, *Technical Manual: Maintenance Data Documentation*, Secretary of the Air Force, September 5, 2019, p. L-11.

[27] TO 00-20-2, 2019, p. G-1.

[28] Slay et al., 1996.

the supply system experiences an increase in demand at the time a part is removed from the aircraft and the replacement part is reordered, and this should be counted.

TO 00-20-2 provides the maintenance record filtering algorithm to extract only those maintenance records that deal with inherent failures, induced failures, and no defect actions. We adhered to this algorithm when requesting data from LIMS-EV. (Please refer to the "Failure Filtering Algorithm" section of this appendix for a reproduction of the filtering algorithm.)

Data Cleaning

After applying the filters to the maintenance record data in the Aerospace Veh Maintenance Doc_New database, a list of all relevant maintenance records with failure data was extracted for inherent failure, induced failure, and no defect actions. We took additional actions to clean these data, described in the "Vehicle Configuration Database" section.

We discovered that some rows of each set of data appeared to have repeating Job Control Numbers (JCNs), as well as repeating WUCs. The JCN is a nine-digit code, of which the first five digits are made up of the Julian date and the last four digits made up of an alphanumeric code serializing the maintenance action. WUCs are codes that provide the hierarchical breakdown of the system, subsystem, and component on which the maintenance work is being conducted. Multiple failures can occur on a single JCN. We filtered the data for unique JCN/WUC combinations and treated multiple failures on a part as a single failure, since it triggers a single demand for a spare.

Additionally, all WUCs beginning with a zero coincided with a scheduled inspection or maintenance activity, which can be excluded from the overall failure count.

After applying these additional filters, failure data were extracted as a count of rows for each of the inherent failure, induced failure, and no defect actions datasets. Joining these three datasets forms a single dataset: total failures for all WUCs, which can be linked back to their respective NIINs for a given MDS.

Linking Flying Hours

The total failures data contain the MDS, aircraft serial numbers, WUCs, NIINs, maintenance action codes, and maintenance time stamps (the start and end of a maintenance action). If these failure instances by date can be linked to a respective operating time, a per-NIIN failure rate can be calculated. Fortunately, the LIMS-EV data source Weapon Systems View through the USAF portal can be used to pull aircraft flight history data, which provide flight hours per calendar day for each aircraft serial number. We pulled all years within these data and linked them to total failures via MDS and aircraft serial number.

This last data link allowed us to calculate empirical failure rates for any NIIN for a given MDS. For the A-10C, we obtained 10,851 failures across the 110 parts on the list of NIINs within the AFSC RSP data. For the rest of this appendix, we refer to these data as the *parts failure data*.

Vehicle Configuration Database

Given the relative scarcity of part failures for the A-10C, we cleaned the Aerospace Veh Configuration database from our LIMS-EV pull. This database provided the link between part numbers and WUC codes and documented part installation and removal dates across the 110 RSP NIINs. From these dates, we calculated the number of flying hours, the number of sorties, and the number of days each part was in use before removal. After cleaning and removing missing entries, obtained 90,985 relevant maintenance entries.

These data would have been very desirable for analysis, but we concluded that they describe different maintenance events. Cross-referencing these data against the *parts failure data* (via the Aerospace Veh Maintenance Doc_New database) revealed no common join key: We could not match the data with unique WUC/serial number combinations. As a result, we excluded this database from our analysis and leveraged the *parts failure data* instead.

Failure Filtering Algorithm

From TO 00-20-2, we used the following filtering algorithm in LIMS-EV to pull the relevant failure data:

> INHERENT FAILURES (TYPE 1)
>
> if the on-equipment
>
> the first position of the WUC is not equal to "0" and . . .
>
> the HOW MAL CLASS equals 1 and
>
> the ACTION TAKEN CODE equals "F,""K," "L," or "Z"
>
> then add UNITS to INHERENT FAILURES.
>
> If the on-equipment
>
> the first position of the WUC is not equal to "0" . . .
>
> the HOW MAL CLASS equals 1 and
>
> the ACTION TAKEN CODE equals "P" or "R" and
>
> there is no related off-equipment record
>
> whose WUC equals this on-equipment record's WUC and
>
> the ACTION TAKEN CODE equals "B"
>
> then add UNITS to INHERENT FAILURES.
>
> If the on-equipment
>
> the first position of the WUC is not equal to "0"
>
> the HOW MAL CLASS equals 1 and

the type of equipment is equal to "E" and

the ACTION TAKEN CODE equals "A"

then add UNITS to INHERENT FAILURES.

INDUCED FAILURES (TYPE 2)

if the on-equipment

the first position of the WUC is not equal to "0" and . . .

(the HOW MAL CLASS equals 2 and

the ACTION TAKEN CODE equals "F,""G," "K," "L," or "Z") or

(the HOW MAL CLASS equals 1 and the ACTION TAKEN CODE equals "G")

then add UNITS to INDUCED FAILURES.

If the on-equipment

the first position of the WUC is not equal to "0" and

the HOW MAL CLASS equals 2 and

the ACTION TAKEN CODE equals "P" or "R" and

there is no related off-equipment record

whose WUC equals this on-equipment record's WUC and

the ACTION TAKEN CODE equals "B"

then add UNITS to INDUCED FAILURES.

If the on-equipment

the first position of the WUC is not equal to "0" and

the HOW MAL CLASS equals 2 and

the type of equipment is equal to "E" and

the ACTION TAKEN CODE equals "A"

then add UNITS to INDUCED FAILURES.

NO DEFECT ACTIONS (TYPE 6)

if the on-equipment

the first position of the WUC is not equal to "0" and . . .

there is a related off-equipment record

whose WUC equals this on-equipment record's WUC and

the ACTION TAKEN CODE equals "B"

then add UNITS to NO DEFECT ACTIONS.

If the on-equipment

the first position of the WUC is not equal to "0" and

(the HOW MAL CLASS equals 6 and the ACTION TAKEN CODE

equals "P," "R,""L,""Z," "T," "S," or "G") or

(the ACTION TAKEN CODE equals "E,""H," "J," "Q," "W,""V,""X," or "Y")

then add UNITS to NO DEFECT ACTIONS.

If the on-equipment

TYPE EQUIPMENT is equal to "E" and

the first position of the WUC is not equal to "0" and

the HOW MAL CLASS equals 6 and

the ACTION TAKEN CODE equals "A"

then add UNITS to NO DEFECT ACTIONS.[29]

LIMS-EV Data Glossary

In this section, we provide definitions using TO 00-20-2 for common LIMS-EV acronyms mentioned in this report.

- *Work unit code*: provides "the hierarchical breakdown of the systems and subsystems for [maintenance data documentation] reporting."[30]
- *How Malfunction Class (HOW MAL CLASS)*: indicates the type of defect of a How Malfunction Code as follows:

    Type 1—Inherent, an actual failure of the item.

    Type 2—Induced, the failure of the item was caused by an outside influence.

    Type 6—No defect, no actual failure.[31]

- *Action Taken Code On Equipment (ATC On)*: "The ATC consists of one character and is used to identify the maintenance action that was taken, such as the removal and replacement of a

---

[29] TO 00-20-2, 2019, p. L-9–L-11.

[30] TO 00-20-2, 2019, p. 10-2.

[31] TO 00-20-2, 2019, p. G-1.

component." *On equipment* signifies "data documented to describe maintenance performed on assemblies, subassemblies, or components [**installed**] to an end item of equipment.[32]

- *Action Taken Code Off Equipment (ATC Off):* "The ATC consists of one character and is used to identify the maintenance action that was taken, such as the removal and replacement of a component. *Off equipment* "signifies data documented to describe maintenance performed on assemblies, subassemblies, or components **removed** from an end item of equipment."[33]

- *Type Equipment Code (TEC):* A four-character alphanumeric code that identifies the end item of equipment on which work is performed. Categories of equipment are identified by the first character of the TEC.[34]

---

[32] TO 00-20-2, 2019, pp. 3-1, 4-10.

[33] TO 00-20-2, 2019, pp. 3-1, 4-10.

[34] See "Table 6-1. Type Equipment Codes," TO 00-20-2, 2019, p. 6-7.

Exploratory Analysis Using Days to Failure as a Predictor of Failure

Using the vehicle configuration data described in Appendix A, we obtained an install date and removal date for many parts in the A-10C RSP kit. This allowed us to calculate the number of failures for the part (within the dataset and within the years in the dataset), the number of total flight hours, the average days of failure per year, and the average flight hours until failure per year. In this appendix, we present some of our exploratory findings with the days-to-failure aspect of these data. (Some numbers and percentages might be marginally different than previously discussed when analyzing these data because there are two actual datasets. Regardless, the analysis comes to the same general conclusion: Most parts failure demand should not be modeled as Poisson-distributed.)

Recall that we could not match these data to our parts failure data, but testing days to failure was only possible with this dataset. Given the exploratory nature of this analysis, we disregarded this discrepancy and assumed that the data document part failures. We also assumed that many of these entries indicated removal due to scheduled maintenance (and, therefore, a part that had reached the end of its life).

First, we evaluated the appropriateness of the Poisson distribution. We estimated the number of days to failure for each part using the average number of days to failure for each part given in the data. We then used the KS test to compare the empirical data against the Poisson distribution and assessed the Poisson goodness of fit.

Second, we trained a neural network to predict part failures based on age. We compared this neural network against the Poisson distribution estimates. In this analysis, we looked at predicting days to failure given previous days to failure data (neural network) and previous average days to failure (Poisson).

Poisson Versus Empirical via the Kolmogorov-Smirnov Test

These data contained an initial installation date and a removal date. There were a total of 91,346 instances of part failures for a total of 104 unique part numbers after filtering the data. Because we were calculating the number of days to failure, we had to drop rows for which there was no removal date because this would imply the number of days to failure for that instance would be zero or infinity, consequently limiting our analysis. As a result, approximately 26.06 percent of the data was lost, which is not negligible but still well within the ability to conduct this analysis.

After calculating the number of days to failure for each instance, we then grouped the part data by unique part number and added all the days in each instance. We then divided this sum by total years in service in the data, thus yielding the average number of days to failure per year for that specific part.

For a specific part, we used this average as our input into the Poisson distribution to calculate a Poisson cumulative distribution function (CDF), which shows the number of days to failure and the probability of the part failing after that specific number of days on the aircraft. We conducted the Poisson CDF calculation for the other 103 parts in this dataset.

To assess the Poisson goodness of fit, we compared the empirical cumulative distribution function (ECDF) of the data for each part with the Poisson CDFs. We used the KS test for goodness of fit, which compared the closeness of the two CDFs. It measures the maximum distance between the two CDFs and compares this distance with its table of values, ultimately culminating in a test statistic and a p-value. We compared this p-value with the alpha = 0.05, giving us a 95-percent confidence interval. The hypothesis tests are as follows:

- H_0: The underlying sample data come from a population that is Poisson-distributed.
- H_A: The underlying sample data *do not* come from a population that is Poisson-distributed.

To calculate the KS test statistic and p-value for each of the 104 parts, we did the following:

1. For each part, we created an ECDF using all empirical data, which is simply a list of days-to-failure instances for that part.
2. For this same part, from that list of days to failure and the total time in service for that part, we calculated the Poisson CDF. The range that we used for the Poisson CDF was from the minimum number of days to failure to the maximum number of days to failure for that specific part.
3. The p-value was then calculated and compared with our selected 0.05 level.

After conducting this process for each part, we found that for this dataset, 5.77 percent (6 of 104) of the parts had errors and were unanalyzable (a mean of 0 or the mean was equal to the minimum and maximum ranges of the data). Of the analyzable parts, 93.88 percent rejected the null hypothesis for the KS test (i.e., sample days to failure data did not come from a distribution that was Poisson-distributed).

Neural Network Versus Poisson

We conducted an 80/20 training and testing split for the data after we preprocessed and scaled the data. The neural network has a batch normalization layer, a rectified linear unit input layer, ten hidden rectified linear unit layers, and a linear output layer. Each layer has 256 nodes except for the output layer, which outputs the neural network's prediction.

After training and testing the neural network, we used the testing data averages to get the Poisson CDF and the 75-percent chance to failure. We chose to change our percentage to 75 percent because this further improved Poisson estimates. (This change did not affect the KS analysis and conclusions because the KS analysis looked at the *entire* Poisson CDF and ECDF.)

The scatterplot in Figure B.1 shows the neural network versus the Poisson estimates. The x-axis shows the actual days until part failure and the y-axis is the prediction. The closer the data points are to the red line, the more accurate the prediction.

Figure B.1. Scatterplot of Predicted Days Versus True Days to Failure (All Data)

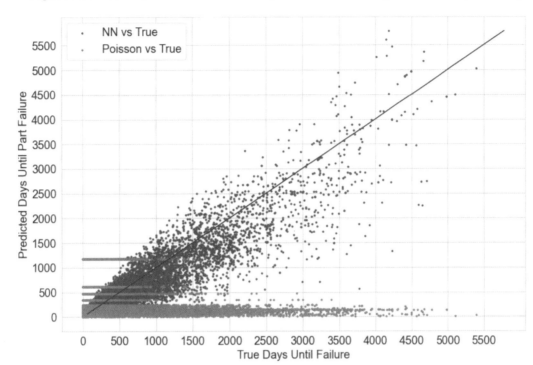

NOTE: NN = neural network.

As shown in Figure B.1, the neural network's predictions are aligning with the red diagonal line, whereas the Poisson predictions are not.

Last, we conducted a mathematical comparison looking at how well these estimates performed given different boundaries. For example, what percentage of estimates for both models were within seven days of the true days to failure? (*Within* includes both the days ahead and behind the prediction.) Table B.1 shows the results.

Table B.1. Boundary Comparison: Days to Failure

Boundary (± Days)	Neural Network Estimate	Poisson Estimate
0 (exact)	0.00%	0.12%
7	3.55%	1.28%
30	16.17%	5.00%
60	**37.12%**	**10.83%**
90	**61.39%**	**17.64%**
180	77.57%	33.60%

Although 90 days is quite a long time, if a logistics commander were given these neural network estimates, they could take those estimates and replace parts at or slightly before the estimate suggests and around 60 percent of the parts will have been replaced within 90 days of failure. This neural network might not be practical, since we would likely need a much higher percentage for RSP kits to ensure battle readiness (we used a more precise LSTM model later), but this shows that even a standard neural network significantly outperforms the Poisson estimates using days to failure. In general, the neural network **outperforms the Poisson estimates by a factor of 2 or greater** in almost all these cases.

We conducted the same analysis using flying hours as the prediction, training the neural network on days to failure, sorties to failure, and ordinal part number. The results are shown in Table B.2.

Table B.2. Boundary Comparison: Flying Hours to Failure

Boundary (± Flying Hours)	Neural Network Estimate (%)	Poisson Estimate (%)
0 (exact)	0.00%	0.03%
10,000	8.86%	3.23%
30,000	23.89%	8.75%
50,000	**40.65%**	**15.44%**
70,000	**67.73%**	**21.94%**
100,000	75.81%	31.12%

Limitations

We trained and tested the neural network on data for parts that we *know* have failed. For example, the first neural network used flying hours and sorties *until failure* to predict days to failure. Ideally, a commander would like to be able to train and test a neural network on these metrics in real time but not to the point of 100 percent of failure. Further analysis can be done by using these two neural network and Poisson models on parts that have yet to fail. For example, if the neural network is given a part that currently has 100 flying hours, whether its prediction is close to when it actually fails should be evaluated.

Abbreviations

AFMC	Air Force Materiel Command
AFSC	Air Force Sustainment Center
AI	artificial intelligence
ASM	Aircraft Sustainability Model
CDF	cumulative distribution function
ECDF	empirical cumulative distribution function
ESCAPE	Enterprise Supply Chain Analysis, Planning, and Execution
EXPRESS	Execution and Prioritization of Repair Support System
IMDS	integrated maintenance data system
JCN	Job Control Number
KS	Kolmogorov-Smirnov
LIMS-EV	Logistics, Installations, and Mission Support–Enterprise View
LRU	line-replaceable unit
LSTM	long short-term memory
MAPE	mean average percent error
MDS	mission design series
MICAP	mission impaired capability, awaiting parts
NIIN	National Item Identification Number
NRTS	not repairable this station
RSP	readiness spares package
TO	technical order
TOIMDR	total organizational and intermediate maintenance demand rate
USAF	U.S. Air Force
Veh	vehicle
WMP	War and Mobilization Plan
WRSK	war reserve spares kit
WUC	work unit code

References

Blazer, Douglas J., "Updating Air Force War Planning for Spares Support," *Air Force Journal of Logistics*, Vol. 35, Nos. 3–4, Fall-Winter 2011.

Geist, Edward, Aaron B. Frank, and Lance Menthe, *Understanding the Limits of Artificial Intelligence for Warfighters:* Vol. 4, *Wargames*, RAND Corporation, RR-A1722-4, 2024.

Gray, Stephen D., *Mitigating Growth Cost for Mobility Readiness Spares Packages*, thesis, Air Force Institute of Technology, March 2004.

Marshall, Aarian, "AI Comes to Car Repair, and Body Shop Owners Aren't Happy," *Wired*, April 13, 2021.

Menthe, Lance, Li Ang Zhang, Edward Geist, Joshua Steier, Aaron B. Frank, Eric Van Hegewald, Gary J. Briggs, Keller Scholl, Yusuf Ashpari, and Anthony Jacques, *Understanding the Limits of Artificial Intelligence for Warfighters:* Vol. 1, *Summary*, RR-A1722-1, 2024.

Mills, Patrick, Sarah A. Nowak, Peter Buryk, John G. Drew, Christopher Guo, and Raffaele Vardavas, *Increasing Cost-Effective Readiness for the U.S. Air Force by Reducing Supply Chain Variance: Technical Analysis of Flying Hour Program Variance*, RAND Corporation, RR-2118-AF, 2018. As of September 19, 2022:
https://www.rand.org/pubs/research_reports/RR2118.html

Pyles, Raymond A., and Hyman L. Shulman, *United States Air Force Fighter Support in Operation Desert Storm*, RAND Corporation, MR-468-AF, 1995. As of September 21, 2022:
https://www.rand.org/pubs/monograph_reports/MR468.html

Russell, Lee R., *A Feasibility Analysis on the Air Force Employment of ESCAPE Supply Chain Management Program*, Air Force Institute of Technology, June 2020.

Russell, Stuart, and Peter Norvig, *Artificial Intelligence: A Modern Approach*, 3rd ed., Prentice Hall, 2010.

Sakulich, Timothy J., and George Zeck, *Computation of ECM War Reserve Materiel Spare Requirements*, Air Force Logistics Command, November 1987.

Scholl, Keller, Gary J. Briggs, Li Ang Zhang, and John L. Salmon, *Understanding the Limits of Artificial Intelligence for Warfighters:* Vol. 5, *Mission Planning*, RAND Corporation, RR-A1722-5, 2024.

Sherbrooke, Craig C., *Using Sorties vs. Flying Hours to Predict Aircraft Spares Demand*, AF501LN1, Logistics Management Institute, April 1997.

Slay, F. Michael, Tovey C. Bachman, Robert C. Kline, T. J. O'Malley, Frank L. Eichorn, and Randall M. King, *Optimizing Spares Support: The Aircraft Sustainability Model*, AF501MR1, Logistics Management Institute, October 1996.

Steier, Joshua, Erik Van Hegewald, Anthony Jacques, Gavin S. Hartnett, and Lance Menthe, *Understanding the Limits of Artificial Intelligence for Warfighters:* Vol. 2, *Distributional Shift in Cybersecurity Datasets*, RAND Corporation, RR-A1722-2, 2024.

Technical Order 00-20-2, *Technical Manual: Maintenance Data Documentation*, Secretary of the Air Force, September 5, 2019.

TO—*See* Technical Order.

U.S. Department of Defense, *Supply Chain Metrics Guide*, 2nd ed., 2020.

Wehbe, Leila, and Aaditya Ramdas, "Introduction to Machine Learning," lecture notes, Carnegie Mellon University, Spring 2019.